Readers

Field of Play:
Measuring Distance, Rate, and Time

by Renata Brunner-Jass

Content Consultant
David T. Hughes
Mathematics Curriculum Specialist

NORWOOD HOUSE PRESS
Chicago, IL

Norwood House Press
PO Box 316598
Chicago, IL 60631

For information regarding Norwood House Press, please visit our website at
www.norwoodhousepress.com or call 866-565-2900.

Special thanks to: Heidi Doyle
Production Management: Six Red Marbles
Editors: Linda Bullock and Kendra Muntz
Printed in Heshan City, Guangdong, China. 208N—012013

Library of Congress Cataloging–in-Publication Data

Brunner-Jass, Renata.

   Field of play: measuring distance, rate, and time/by Renata M. Brunner-Jass;
   content consultant, David Hughes.
   p. cm.—(iMath)

   Audience: 10–12.
   Audience: Grade 4 to 6.

   Summary: "The mathematical concepts of distance, rate, and time are explored
   as students partake in their school's annual field day. Readers also learn
   about proportions, ratios, and cross products. This book includes a discovery
   activity, connections to science and engineering, and mathematical vocabulary
   introduction"—Provided by publisher.

Includes bibliographical references and index.

ISBN 978-1-59953-571-5 (library edition: alk. paper)
ISBN 978-1-60357-540-9 (ebook)

1. Mathematics—Study and teaching (Elementary) 2. Distances—Measurement—Juvenile literature.
3. Time measurements—Juvenile literature. 4. Speed—Measurement—Juvenile literature. I. Title.

QA40.5.B78 2012
530.8—dc23
2012031020

CONTENTS

Note to Caregivers:

Throughout this book, many questions are posed to the reader. Some are open-ended and ask what the reader thinks. Discuss these questions with your child and guide him or her in thinking through the possible answers and outcomes. There are also questions posed which have a specific answer. Encourage your child to read through the text to determine the correct answer. Most importantly, encourage answers grounded in reality while also allowing imaginations to soar. Information to help support you as you share the book with your child is provided in the back in the **Additional Notes** section.

Bold words are defined in the glossary in the back of the book.

4

Field Day!

Field Day is a tradition at our school. It happens on the Saturday before the last week of school, marking the end of another year.

Planning starts months ahead. Students and teachers meet weekly after school to be sure the day is a huge success. Ms. Henry, the P.E. teacher, is always on the committee. There would be no Field Day without her.

Fifteen students and four teachers served on the committee this year. That made the **ratio** of teachers to students 4 to 15. The ratio can be written other ways, as well. One way is $4:15$. Another is $\frac{4}{15}$. A ratio compares two numbers or measures through division.

The word *wacky* kept coming up in discussion. The crazier the activities, the better. Members of the committee interviewed activity leaders at the community center and did some online research to plan games that were inexpensive, fun, and open to everyone.

Read on to see just how wacky it got!

Planning for the Big Day

Before the Field Day, Ms. Henry helped her student volunteers prepare for their jobs. She gave each one of them a stopwatch and showed them how to use it to measure time. Event managers wore yellow vests and timekeepers wore red vests.

She also gave them tape measures. For measuring practice, they worked in pairs to measure the lengths of the lines painted on the floor of the basketball court.

"Now," Ms. Henry began, "let's review finding rates. A **rate** is a special kind of ratio. It compares two amounts that aren't measured the same way. Say, for example, you run from one wall of the gym to another, tag the wall, and run back again. Say that's 180 feet in all, and you run it in 30 seconds."

"You can use that information to find out how fast you run per second. In other words, you can find your **unit rate**. And there are different ways you can do that."

Idea 1: You can use a **double number line** to model the distance you traveled to the wall and back again and the total time it took.

The distance you ran was 180 feet, and your time was 30 seconds.

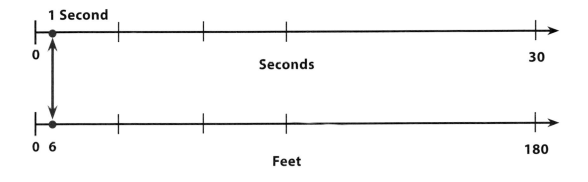

Look for the relationship between the number lines. If you run 180 feet in 30 seconds, how far do you run in 1 second? The answer is the unit rate. You write it as a fraction with a denominator of 1.

Do you think modeling with double number lines is a useful way to find a unit rate? Why or why not?

Idea 2: You can use a **table** to find how many feet you ran per second. Begin by writing the time it took to run a distance of 180 feet. Think about the relationship between seconds and feet. Observe that, if you change one, you change the other. In this case, you want to find a unit rate. So, you want to know how many feet you traveled per second.

Seconds	Feet
30	180
15	90
5	30
1	6

Do you think using a table is a useful way to find a unit rate? Why or why not?

Idea 3: Use a **proportion** to find two equal ratios. A proportion is an **equation** that shows two **equivalent** fractions. An equation is a number sentence that shows that two mathematical expressions are equal. Equivalent fractions have the same value.

You can use **cross products** to solve a proportion. That is, you can multiply the numerator of each fraction by the denominator of the other fraction. When you have two equivalent ratios, the cross products are equal.

You ran 180 feet in 30 seconds. But how many feet is that per second? Let the letter x stand for the number of feet you're trying to find.

Use what you know to write an equation.

$$\frac{180}{30} = \frac{x}{1}$$

Then, use cross products to find the value of x.

$30 \times x = 180 \times 1$

$30x = 180$

$x = 6$

$$\frac{180 \text{ ft}}{30 \text{ seconds}} = \frac{6 \text{ ft}}{\text{second}}$$

Do you think setting up and using cross products to solve a proportion is a useful way to find a unit rate? Why or why not?

Wind 'Em Up!

Do this activity with a friend. Collect some wind-up toys. Build a chart. The chart should have one column for each wind-up toy. Inside the column for each toy, write a ratio that compares how far each toy travels (measured in inches or centimeters) to how much time (in seconds) it takes to travel that distance.

Use tape to make a starting line and a finish line on a flat surface, such as a table. While one of you winds a toy and releases it from behind the starting line, the other uses a stopwatch or a watch with a second hand to time how long it takes for the toy to either reach the finish line or stop entirely.

This measurement of time will be the denominator in your ratio.

Now, measure the distance the toy traveled. Measure to the nearest whole number. Write this measurement as the numerator in your ratio.

Find the toy's unit rate of travel. Repeat the activity using all of the wind-up toys.

Decide which method you will use to find the unit rate.

- Will you use a double number line?
- Will you use a table?
- Will you write and use cross products?

You may want to **round** some numbers to the nearest whole number to make it easier to find approximate unit rates. That is, look one place to the right of the digit you want to round to. If the digit is five or greater, add one to the digit you are rounding. If the digit to the right is less than five, leave the digit you are rounding unchanged.

Examine the unit rates you find. **Order** them from least to greatest. Which toy travels the slowest? Which travels the fastest?

Let the Games Begin!

At many family reunions and sports field days, the egg relay, or egg-in-a-spoon relay, is a tradition. That's probably because the results are so comical.

Most people play by carrying a spoon in one hand. A hard-boiled egg rolls inside the spoon as a racer runs or walks quickly toward a finish line a few feet away.

In this race, the rules were changed. First, racers were told that they had to hold their spoons in their mouths. That would leave their hands free, but they couldn't touch their spoons or eggs. If they did, they were disqualified.

Second, racers had to race backward. This rule definitely made the race harder, as racers craned their necks to see where they were going. Eggs soon began to roll off of spoons, and only two people managed to reach the finish line. The winner raced 60 feet in 20 seconds. What was the winner's unit rate?

Use a double number line to find the answer.

Keep Rolling

Janice managed the Newspaper Delivery activity. She lined up ten tricycles along a starting line. She put ten folded newspapers along a **parallel** line, 50 yards away. Parallel lines always remain the same distance apart.

"To play this game," Janice said, "you must ride a tricycle down to the line, pick up the newspaper, and ride back to the starting line. If you drop the paper, you must pick it up and then continue pedaling. The first one back to the starting line with the newspaper is the winner."

Riders folded their long legs like hairpins to put their feet on the tricycles' tiny pedals. They jutted out their elbows to grasp the plastic handles.

"Ready. Set. Go!" Janice announced.

The racers pedaled as fast as they could. They hunched over their tricycles. Their knees pumped up and down. The first racer to the line leaned over to grab the newspaper, tucked it under her arm, swung her tricycle around, and started pedaling madly. But the paper kept falling, and she kept stopping to pick it up again.

Other racers tucked their newspapers inside their T-shirts or shorts. One put it in his mouth. That seemed a good decision, because he was the first rider to get back to the starting line. "45 seconds!" called the timekeeper. What was the winner's unit rate to the nearest yard? Use a table to find the answer.

Pass the Torch

Maria managed the Olympic Torch Relay. She kept a box filled with torches at one end of the starting line. She didn't want anyone to see the torches until the race began.

Each relay team had six people. Three lined up at one line. The other three lined up at a parallel line 40 yards away. When the teams were ready, Maria took a torch from the box at her feet.

She held the handle of a rubber plunger in her hand. "This is your torch," she announced. She heard instant groaning from the racers. "Inside each torch is a red wobbling ball of gelatin, or jelly, to represent a flame." The groaning got louder.

"The first torch-holder will run as fast as possible to the other side and pass the torch. Then, the next racer will run back to me. If at any time a racer drops or spills the gelatin, he or she must stop, refill the torch, and then resume racing. The winning team is the team that finishes the race first. Does everyone understand?"

No questions followed, so Maria and the timekeeper distributed the torches. The gelatin wobbled wildly, forcing the racers to balance the plungers carefully. No one wanted to have to pick up the "flame" before the race even began.

Maria blew the whistle, and the players moved forward slowly, still trying to balance their flames. The racers moved much like turtles, one slow step at a time.

"Brian," Maria said to the timekeeper, "time the first part of the relay, would you? I want to get an idea of what rate we can expect for the entire relay."

"Sure," Brian answered, watching the first racers get to the other side. He pressed the stopwatch. "20 seconds," he said.

What was the unit rate for the first racer to reach the opposite side? Use cross products to solve a proportion to find the answer.

Parachute Ball Toss

Terence and Lydia unfolded two silky parachutes across the ground. They put a box filled with tennis balls next to each parachute.

Terence called the first ten players forward. "Space yourselves around the parachute," he told them. "Then, grab the edge of the parachute in your hands and lift."

While those players followed his directions, ten more players grabbed hold of the second parachute. Like the first group, they struggled to lift the heavy fabric.

"We're going to practice before we begin the game," Terrence announced. "Lift and then drop your arms to get some air beneath your parachute. Give it a try."

Both teams struggled at first but soon found a rhythm, or natural movement.

"That's great!" Terence called as Lydia clapped. "You're ready to begin."

Lydia continued. "Terence and I will each stand at a different parachute. We will each toss a tennis ball into your parachutes at the same time. You must work as a team to keep the ball in the air by snapping your parachutes."

"We will continue to toss balls and you must continue to keep them in the air. If a ball falls out of the chute, leave it. When I blow the whistle, let your parachute settle to the ground. The winning team is the team with the most tennis balls still on the parachute. Does everyone understand?"

Everyone nodded in agreement, and the clock began with the first toss of a tennis ball. Lydia and Terence tossed a total of 10 tennis balls in 10 seconds. How many balls did they toss per second?

In the Frying Pan

Logan lay down ten plastic discs at one edge of a playing field. He put one pair of chopsticks on each disc.

Melissa stood opposite Logan, about 50 yards away. She placed ten rubber chickens on the ground. Each rubber chicken corresponded to one disc on the other side.

The first ten players in line claimed a disc. They picked up the chopsticks and waited for directions.

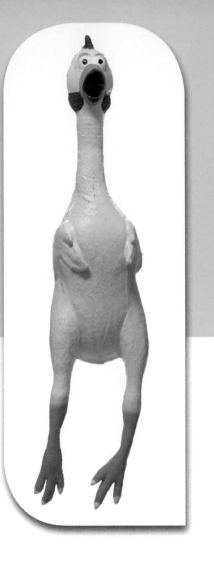

"We want you to think of the disc on which you are standing as a frying pan," Logan explained. "When I blow the whistle, jump from the pan and race to your chicken."

"Use your chopsticks to pick up your chicken. No hands may touch the chicken at any time, or you will be disqualified. Carry the chicken back to where you began and drop it in the frying pan. The first one to do this wins."

"Ready. Set. Go!" Logan called.

The race to the chickens was swift. The race back was a little slower. But, every chicken made it onto a disc, or in other words, "into a frying pan." It took the winner 85 seconds to get his chicken and return home to put it in the frying pan.

How many yards did the winner run per second? Round the answer to the nearest whole number.

18

Ball Balance

Emily lined up 15 extra-long plastic straws along a starting line. Raul placed a table-tennis ball next to each straw. Then, they put up a matching number of plastic cones along a parallel line 40 feet away.

With everything in place, Emily and Raul directed players to claim a straw and practice balancing the table-tennis balls on top of their straws. "You will carry your ball atop your straw to the cone, go around the cone, and then come back to the starting line."

"If," Raul continued, "you drop the ball, stop, pick it up, put it back on your straw, and resume running. The first racer back to the starting line is the winner. Does everyone understand the rules?"

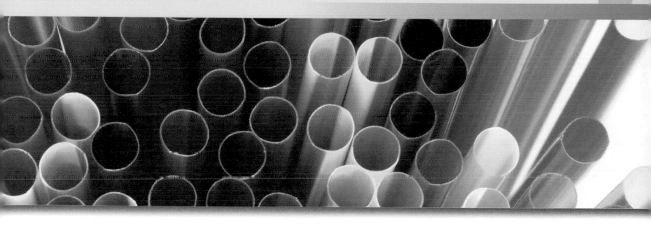

Heads nodded, so Emily blew her whistle. The racers moved forward. The hands holding the straws danced to the left and right, trying to keep their balls from falling. Not everyone was successful. One racer's ball fell beneath the feet of the player to his left. The plastic ball cracked before the racer could reclaim it. Raul dashed forward to offer the racer a new ball.

More balls fell as racers circled around the cones. The winner made it back to the starting line in 75 seconds. How many feet did the racer run per second? Round the answer to the nearest whole number.

Fill the Bucket

Jasmine and a small group of volunteers set up their game near the water truck. First, they placed a line of ten plastic hoops on the ground. Then, they collected 20 buckets. They filled ten buckets with water from the truck. They left the other buckets empty.

They put the buckets holding water inside the hoops. They carried the empty buckets to a parallel line 30 feet away. One volunteer stood by each empty bucket. All of the volunteers wore aprons.

Jasmine organized players into teams, and each team claimed a hoop with its bucket of water. Jasmine gave the first person in each team an apron and a sponge.

"Welcome to the Sponge Relay," she said. "Players will take turns. Each player will put on the apron, fill the sponge with water, and run to the bucket on the opposite side. After squeezing the sponge, the runner will return and pass the sponge and apron to the next runner. The first team to fill the bucket on the other side to the 2-inch mark is the winner. Got it?"

Everyone nodded, and the first runners were already wearing their aprons and ready to go. Jasmine gave the signal, and the game began.

By the time a winner was announced, everyone was soaked. The winners had filled their buckets to the line in 2.5 minutes. What was the fill rate per minute?

Thwack!

Liam's game attracted hockey fans. They watched as he put five colorful discs on the ground and then measured a distance of 52 yards to set up a parallel line of plastic cones.

He organized the people who wanted to play into groups of three and assigned each group to a different disc. Then, he gave a hockey stick to the first player on each team. Next, he opened a box of juggling balls. He put a ball at the feet of each player holding a hockey stick.

"When I blow my whistle," Liam said, "use your hockey stick to move the juggling ball down the field, around the cone, and back. Then, pass your stick to the next player on your team. The first team to finish the relay is the winning team. Ready. Set. Go!"

"Thwack!" Liam listened as players used their sticks to move the balls down the field. The first player to return home made the trip in 52 seconds.

How many yards per minute did the player run?

Hoop It Up

Sarita was a champion hooper, so she asked Ms. Henry if she could be in charge of the Hoop Race. This race was part of the games every year, and it was one of the most popular games.

Forty students and teachers lined up to play. Sarita gave each of them a plastic hoop. "Look straight ahead. You will see a cone 30 feet from where you stand. You must keep the hoop spinning as you move to the cone, go around it, and come back again."

"It's likely to get crowded around the cone, so watch out. If your hoop falls, stop, pick it up, and then continue hooping. Let me show you what I mean."

Sarita spun the hoop around her waist and kept it spinning as she raced to the cone and back. "Do you get the idea?" she asked the players.

There was almost a unanimous yes as players began spinning their hoops. Sarita blew her whistle, and the players moved forward carefully.

Just as Sarita had predicted, the space around the cone became crowded, and hoops bounced against hoops. People were still moving while others bent to pick up their hoops to start again. The result was hilarious. Even the players were laughing.

At last, the winner reached the finish line in 20 seconds. How many feet per second did the player hoop?

Later in the day, Sarita managed another hoop activity. This one didn't require any hooping skills, so more players seemed to be interested. She counted 52 players in all and fetched an equal number of hoops.

The players huddled around Sarita, who stood in the middle of a soccer field. Soccer nets bordered two sides of the field.

Sarita gave four players a hoop. Then, she explained the directions. "Think of the distance between the two nets as the home of the Hoop Sharks, which are hungry beasts eager to catch you in their hoops. If you're caught, you become a new Hoop Shark. Then, come to me, and I'll give you a hoop of your own. Then, run back to the playing field to capture a runner."

"Runners, you must run from this goal line to the opposite goal line without getting caught. Are you ready to run?"

Once the Hoop Sharks were ready, Sarita blew her whistle. The game was on!

One Hoop Shark captured 16 players in 4 minutes. How many players did the Hoop Shark capture per minute?

Pull Harder!

Tara painted a starting line at the edge of a flat field. Next, she fetched ten plastic sleds.

By the time Tara returned to the field, a group of eager participants had assembled. She chose 20 players. Half of them would be sledders, while the other half would be pullers.

Sledders and pullers claimed their sleds. When everyone was in place, Tara explained the directions. "Pullers, it's your job to pull your passenger to the finish line, which is 50 yards from here. Sledders, it's your job to stay on your sled. If you fall off, your team is disqualified. The first sled team to the finish line is the winner."

Tara blew her whistle to start the game.

It took 12 seconds for a team to be disqualified, when the passenger leaned too far to one side soon after the start and caused the sled to tip over.

If the team covered only 9 yards before being disqualified, what was their unit rate of travel?

CONNECTING TO HISTORY

In ancient Egypt 3,000 years ago, children used sticks to push spinning hoops of dried grapevines. They also tossed hoops to one another and spun the hoops around their waists.

As early traders visited new places and met new people, they returned home with new ideas. By the 1300s, hoops became wildly popular in England. Children and adults played with them.

In the 1700s, English sailors reached Hawaii. There, they watched hula dancers perform. The dancers' movements reminded them of spinning hoops. So, the sailors renamed the familiar toy a *hula-hoop*.

In 1957, a company in Australia made wooden hoops for gym classes. By then, Richard Knerr and Arthur Melin had started a toy company called Wham-O. They began to make hoops, too. But they made them from a new plastic.

Knerr and Melin couldn't claim to be the toy's maker because no one will ever know who made the first hoop. But they registered the name with the government. They called the plastic hoop the Hula Hoop®.

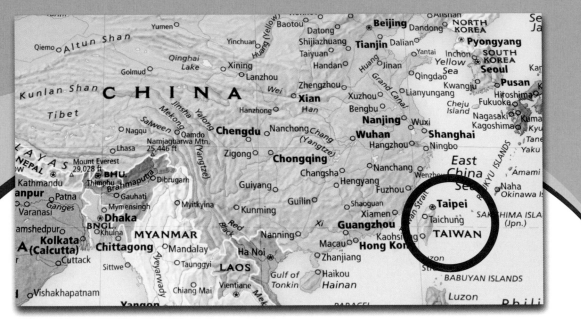

When sales began, a Hula Hoop® sold for $1.98. By the end of the second year of sales, the company had sold more than 100,000,000 hoops. People participated in hooping contests. But they didn't stop there. Many hoop fans created and mastered new tricks and exhibited their talents at public shows.

Hooping didn't stay popular for long, but it has returned in the 21st century as a great form of exercise. Today, people use hoops to do more than simple hooping. They also hoop dance, hoop jump, and hoop roll. They also play Kill the Hoop, a game in which players throw or kick a ball through a hoop.

Many hoopers aren't content to spin alone. They prefer to spin in groups. Sometimes those groups are really large. These hoop-spinning events are called Mass Hoops.

In 2000, hoopers gathered in Kaohsiung, Taiwan, to spin hoops. They set a record, with 2,290 participants spinning successfully all at once. Eleven years later in Taipei City, Taiwan, 2,496 hoopers broke the record, which had stood for a decade.

MATH AT WORK

Have you ever listened to sports television announcers talk about a game? It might be a football or a basketball game. It might be a track meet, where runners speed down short and long distances. Or it might be a gymnastics competition, where players earn scores for their work on balance beams, parallel bars, and rings. Whatever the sport, announcers use math to describe plays and players.

For example, a baseball announcer may give a player's batting average. The announcer needs a variety of data to figure out that average. He starts with the number of hits a player has. Then, he figures out how many times the player was at bat. There are a number of rules about what counts as "at bat." A walk, for example, doesn't count.

Next, the announcer divides the number of hits by the total times at bat. The answer is a decimal number with several places. The announcer rounds the answer to the third decimal point. So, a player may have a batting average of .300, for example.

That batting average tells fans something important. Multiply the average by 100. The result tells you what percentage of times a player actually hits a ball while at bat.

CONNECTING TO SCIENCE

If you live along a coastline, you may hear news of hurricanes coming toward shore. A hurricane is a tropical storm with heavy winds. To qualify as a hurricane, those winds must reach a constant speed of at least 74 miles per hour.

In the **Northern Hemisphere**, where the United States is located, the winds move counterclockwise around an eye, or calm center. This eye is usually 20 to 30 miles wide. However, eyes can be hundreds of miles wide.

Hurricanes bring heavy winds, heavy rains, flooding, and **surges**. A surge is a huge swell of water that rises as much as 20 feet above the ocean's surface and travels toward land with the tide. It is the surge that often harms the most people and destroys the most land.

Meteorologists are weather scientists. They keep the public informed about every kind of weather, including dangerous storms such as hurricanes.

This image shows a radar weather station. Meteorologists shoot short bursts of radio waves toward objects in the sky. The objects reflect the radio waves, and radar antennae at the station pick them up. Computers inside the station process the information the antennae receive to determine the velocity of a weather system.

Meteorologists report a hurricane's speed, but the hurricane's direction is far more important. To be prepared, people need to know the storm's velocity, meaning the storm's speed and direction. A hurricane with a velocity of 120 miles per hour north is a greater threat to people living in that direction. However, hurricanes can change direction. That's why meteorologists collect data from different sources. They get photographs from weather **satellites** 22,000 feet above Earth. They get data from aircraft that fly into the storm, and they get more data from **radar** systems on the ground.

In the United States, the hurricane season is from June 1st through November 30th. The deadliest hurricane in U.S. history occurred in Galveston, Texas, in 1900. The storm surge was 16 feet high, and the winds blew from 130 to 156 miles per hour. More than 6,000 people lost their lives.

The Games Continue

Feather Javelins

Caroline, the timekeeper, helped Sydney paint a starting line across the grass. They painted a parallel line 30 yards away.

Then, Sydney carried a basket of long turkey feathers to the starting line. People soon gathered to participate in the Feather Relay.

"We have enough players to make five teams," Sydney announced. "So, make your teams and claim a spot behind the starting line."

Players scrambled to make their teams and find their places. When everyone was ready, Sydney explained the game.

"This is a relay race. Think of yourselves as Olympic **javelin** throwers. And think of this," she said, holding up a feather for people to see, "as your javelin. You will throw your feather javelin as far as you can. When it lands, pick it up and throw it again. Throw to the line, turn around, and come back to where you started. Then, pass your feather to the next runner. Are you ready?"

The first runners were ready to throw their feather javelins as soon as Sydney blew her whistle. The feathers flew off course, and runners crossed paths to pick them up and throw again. It took two minutes for the first runner to reach the starting line again.

How many yards per minute did the runner travel?

30

Blowpipes

Jarrod organized players into teams of ten. Team members then organized again. Five members stood behind one line. The remaining five members moved behind a parallel line 75 feet away.

"This is the equipment you need to run this relay," Jarrod explained, holding up a paper-towel tube and a table-tennis ball. "Think of the tube as a blow pipe. Let me show you how this relay will work."

Jarrod got on his hands and knees and faced the opposite line. He placed the table-tennis ball in front of him. Then, he put the tube to his mouth and blew. As the ball moved forward, so did Jarrod. All the while, he blew as hard as he could through the tube.

"That's all you have to do," Jarrod said, as he stood up and brushed grass off of his legs. He saw participants shaking their heads gently, laughing at how difficult this relay was going to be.

"Get ready!" Lynn, the timekeeper, yelled. "Set. Go!" The first players fell to the ground and began blowing as hard as they could.

What followed was too funny for words. Jarrod and Lynn laughed as they encouraged racers to blow harder. It took 120 seconds for a player to reach the opposite line.

How many feet per second did the player travel?

Put It On!

Babette volunteered to manage the Put It On! relay. She had played the game herself in last year's Field Day. She had laughed so hard that it had hurt. She looked forward to laughing that hard again today.

Long before today's event, Babette and other members of the planning committee began collecting clothing and old suitcases. They kept tallies of everything they collected to know how many teams could play in the relay.

Items	Tallies	Totals
Shirts	𝍷𝍷𝍷 𝍷𝍷𝍷 ||	12
Pants	𝍷𝍷𝍷 𝍷𝍷𝍷	10
Skirts	𝍷𝍷𝍷 𝍷𝍷𝍷 |	11
Hats	𝍷𝍷𝍷 𝍷𝍷𝍷 |||	13
Pairs of Gloves	𝍷𝍷𝍷 𝍷𝍷𝍷	10
Pairs of Socks	𝍷𝍷𝍷 𝍷𝍷𝍷 𝍷𝍷𝍷 𝍷𝍷𝍷 |	21
Scarves	𝍷𝍷𝍷 𝍷𝍷𝍷 |	11
Belts	𝍷𝍷𝍷 𝍷𝍷𝍷 𝍷𝍷𝍷	15
Suitcases	𝍷𝍷𝍷 𝍷𝍷𝍷	10

On the day of the game, Babette and Jaime, the timekeeper, filled 10 suitcases. Each suitcase had one of every clothing item in their chart except socks. They put two pairs of socks in every suitcase.

Babette and Jaime placed all of the filled suitcases 35 yards from the starting line. Then, Jaime organized teams while Babette explained the rules.

"You will each race to the suitcase and put on every item of clothing you find inside. If an item is too small, such as a shirt, don't worry. You can wear it on your head, or anywhere else you choose. The only rule is that you put on every item of clothing."

"Jaime and I will stand by the suitcases. When you have put on all of your clothes, signal one of us. We'll check your suitcase. When we give you the okay, remove all of the clothes you've put on and put them back in the suitcase. Then, run back to the starting line to tag the next runner. Any questions?"

There were none, so Babette blew her whistle. The race was on!

Babette and Jaime gave a special award to the fastest dresser. He put on every item of clothing in 9 seconds. About how many items did he put on per second? (Hint: pairs of gloves and pairs of socks count as one item each.)

What's the Challenge?

Roberto and Mirabelle spent hours thinking of challenges for the participants in the Challenge Yourself race. Their final list included:

- Do a handstand. Stay upright for 3 seconds.
- Do two somersaults.
- Say the last ten letters of the alphabet backwards.
- Cut out a circle from construction paper.
- Unwind the rubber band ball. Then, rewind it.
- Put the beads on the string. Then, take them off again.
- Peel an orange and put the fruit in the bowl.
- Copy the word written on the bag.
- Use the camera to snap a self-portrait.
- Write a fortune for a fortune cookie.

 Did You Know?

People have argued for some time about who invented fortune cookies. Do they come from Japan or China? Or are they an American invention?

Although the cookies come at the end of a meal in Chinese restaurants in the United States, the first fortune cookies probably came from Japan. A Japanese print made in 1878 shows a baker making fortune cookies. The cookies, like those that bakers in Japan bake today, are larger and browner than the cookies diners eat in the United States, and the paper fortune is outside the cookie, tucked in the cookie's fold.

They wrote the directions for each challenge on large cards. Then, they gathered the supplies needed for some of the challenges.

Next, they set up ten folding tables 20 yards from a starting line. They put supplies on each table, along with sets of directions.

When everything was ready, Mirabelle chose the first ten players. They stood at the starting line, ready to run.

Roberto explained the rules. "When you reach the table, read the directions you find there. Then, complete the challenge. When you've done everything the challenge asked you to do, run back. The winner of each round will play in a run-off challenge."

"Get ready. Set. Go!" The runners were on their way.

The winner of the run-off ran 20 yards, completed the challenge, and returned in 16 seconds. What distance did she run per second?

Cone Slalom

Ms. Henry took responsibility for creating a racecourse. She made the race more difficult by using large traffic cones as obstacles. Runners would have to **slalom**, or zigzag, around the cones, like skiers around poles. But they had to do it on one foot.

The course's total distance was 200 yards, a real workout. But that didn't prevent lots of people from standing in line, waiting to race.

More than 50 racers completed the course. The fastest player completed the course in 3 minutes 20 seconds. What distance did the player travel per second?

Did You Know?

Dennis Oppenheim was an artist best known for creating installation art. Installation art is three-dimensional art that fills a certain space and changes the way people see that space.

In 2007, Oppenheim used traffic cones to create installation art in the United States and in South Korea. Each installation used five traffic cones. The cones stood more than 16-feet (5 meters) tall.

CONNECTING TO ENGINEERING

Workers in New York City began using traffic cones in 1914. Those cones, invented by American Charles P. Rudabaker, were made of concrete.

Decades later, officials in Britain used traffic cones that burned paraffin, a waxy product made from wood and petroleum. Petroleum is drilled from the ground and is the source of gasoline.

David Morgan of Britain claimed to build the first plastic traffic cones. Those cones replaced wooden cones shaped like pyramids.

In modern times, manufacturers make traffic cones from rubber and from brightly colored **thermoplastics**. A thermoplastic softens when it is heated and then hardens when it cools. Manufacturers also make traffic cones from recycled plastic bottles. And not all cones are cones at all. Some are moveable **cylinders**.

Today, most traffic cones come in bright orange or lime green. They often have striping around them that reflects light from a car's headlights. Together, the bright colors and striping make the cones easy to see.

Field Day Winds Down

Melt Faster!

Ms. Henry arranged for an ice company to deliver ten 15-pound blocks of ice for the Look What's Melting game.

Ms. Henry assigned one team to each block of ice. "When I blow my whistle," Ms. Henry said, "your team will work together to melt the block of ice as quickly as you can. The first team to melt the entire block is the winner."

The whistle blew, and team members began rubbing, hugging, fanning, and blowing on their blocks. It took half an hour for one block of ice to melt completely. How many pounds of ice melted per minute?

? Did You Know?

Salt lowers the temperature at which water freezes. It also lowers the temperature at which it melts.

Imagine sprinkling an ice cube with salt. The salt **dissolves** in the part of the cube that melts first. The salty water touches more ice, lowering the melting temperature. That's why in cold climates people often throw salt onto icy sidewalks. The sooner the ice disappears, the safer the sidewalks are to walk on!

Mail Truck

Mr. Gomez, a new teacher at our school, ran the Mail Truck event. Before the event began, a troop of volunteers helped him set things up.

Volunteers painted two parallel lines 80 yards apart. They put ten wheelbarrows along the starting line. Then, they laid cardboard boxes along each path toward the finish line. The boxes were all different sizes, from small to huge.

Mr. Gomez explained the directions to the players standing by their wheelbarrows. "Think of your wheelbarrow as a mail truck. Your job is to pick up and deliver the mail," he said. "You see the mail in front of you. It's the series of boxes leading to the post office, or finish line. You must stop to pick up each box. The boxes must stay in your truck at all times. If any box falls out, stop to put it back in again. Then, continue to the finish line."

Mr. Gomez yelled, "Ready. Set. Go!" The postal workers got to work.

Balancing the large boxes slowed many of the players. It took four minutes for the winner to reach the finish line. What distance did the winner travel per minute?

Catch of the Day

Three teachers managed the Fish Net activity. Weeks before Field Day, they made four enormous fishing nets from netting usually used in insect nets. Each net required four players to hold the corners.

On Field Day, the teachers painted an area 50 yards wide and 50 yards long on the grass. Student activity managers held the fishing nets. They also wore fishing hats and boots.

"We're ready to begin fishing," Mr. Gomez called. "Line up, everyone!"

Players stood around Mr. Gomez as he explained the game. "From this moment on, consider yourself a fish. When I blow my whistle, you are free to enter the playing field. The fishers will attempt to capture you in their nets. If you're caught, you must stay in the net and run along as the fishers who caught you try to catch more fish. You may not run outside the playing field. The first player to reach the opposite side without being caught is the winner.

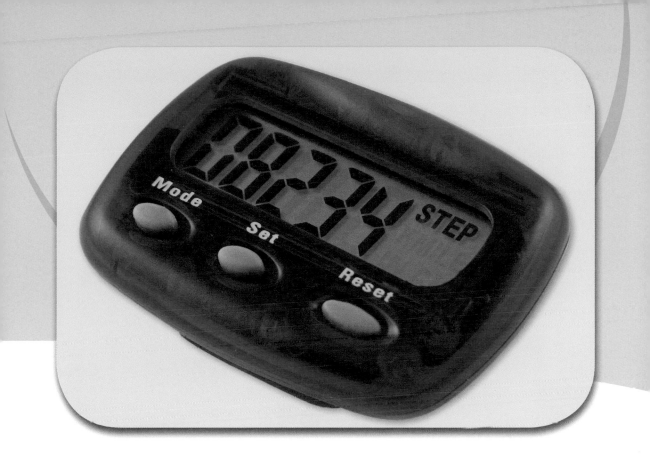

"Before we begin, we're going to tag each fish. That means we're going to ask you to wear a pedometer. A pedometer measures the number of steps you take. We're going to count each step you take as a foot. We want to know how far each of you travels to escape the nets."

Mr. Gomez looked around. Every fish wore a pedometer. "Get ready, fishers," he yelled to the volunteers on the field. "Here come the fish!" The fish swarmed onto the field.

The only person to escape the fishers and cross the finish line traveled about 80 yards in 2 minutes 40 seconds.

How many yards per second did the fish travel?

After all of the winners had their ribbons, and after all of the reporters and photographers from the local newspapers had left, members of the planning committee began cleaning up. There were empty water bottles to collect from the fields and P.E. equipment to pick up and store.

Mr. Gomez had brought a box of pedometers from his last event into the meeting room. "Mr. Gomez," Jaime asked, "may I borrow a pedometer? I think I've walked a dozen miles today. I'd like to know how many more miles I'm going to walk before the fields are clean."

Logan and Sarita wanted to know, too. Mr. Gomez gave each of them a pedometer. They wore their pedometers as they traveled across fields, in and out of the gym, and through school buildings. After three hours, they stopped to compare distances.

	Pedometer Recording
Jaime	10,560 feet
Sarita	21,120 feet
Logan	15,240 feet

"I wonder," Logan said, "how much distance we covered per hour?"

Sarita and Jaime thought about the strategies they could use to find out.

Idea 1: They could use **double number lines** to find how many miles each of them had traveled per hour. "This is a good strategy," said Sarita, "but drawing accurate number lines can take a long time. There must be a faster way to find the answer."

Idea 2: They could use a **table** to find how many miles each of them traveled per hour. "I like using tables," said Jaime, "but only when the numbers are small. These numbers are large. It might take a long time to figure out a relationship between the numbers. That's often a problem with this strategy."

Idea 3: They could use a **proportion**. Logan spoke up. "This strategy is my favorite. It's easy to do. It's a faster way to an answer, and you don't need any special materials. All you need to remember is to use cross products to find the answer. I say we use this one."

What distance did each student cover per hour? How will you find out?

Jaime and Sarita solved their proportions first. Then, they waited until Logan was finished. How many feet per hour did Logan walk?

Jaime

$$\frac{10{,}560 \text{ feet}}{3 \text{ hours}} = \frac{x \text{ feet}}{\text{hour}}$$

$3 \times x = 10{,}560 \times 1$

$3x = 10{,}560$

$x = 3{,}520 \text{ feet}$

$$\frac{10{,}560 \text{ feet}}{3 \text{ hours}} = \frac{3{,}520 \text{ feet}}{\text{hour}}$$

Sarita

$$\frac{21{,}120 \text{ feet}}{3 \text{ hours}} = \frac{x \text{ feet}}{\text{hour}}$$

$3 \times x = 21{,}120 \times 1$

$3x = 21{,}120$

$x = 7{,}040 \text{ feet}$

$$\frac{21{,}120 \text{ feet}}{3 \text{ hours}} = \frac{7{,}040 \text{ feet}}{\text{hour}}$$

Logan

$$\frac{15{,}240 \text{ feet}}{3 \text{ hours}} = \frac{x \text{ feet}}{\text{hour}}$$

How many feet per hour did Logan walk?

Field Day was a huge success. It was so successful, in fact, that Jaime, Sarita, and Logan agreed to be part of the planning committee again next year. Their challenge, they decided, was to make next year's games even wackier.

WHAT COMES NEXT?

Imagine yourself on the planning committee for a Field Day at your school. Your assignment is to build an obstacle course for students ages 12 and up. You will set up the course on a soccer field.

Begin by visiting the field. Take paper to sketch the site. Is it flat? Are there any holes or bare patches in the ground that could create problems?

What borders the field? Is there a running track? Is there a wild area? Look out for safety hazards. Include them in your sketch so that you know which areas to work around.

List the equipment you will use to create obstacles. The equipment must be sturdy and safe. Also, think about how you can use this equipment. The course should be for people with a wide range of abilities.

The students who created this obstacle course used hay bales and a horse they made themselves.

Order the obstacles from easiest to most challenging. Map them on your design.

Discuss your design with a P.E. teacher or someone else who has experience building obstacle courses. Revise your design based on what you learn.

Then, if your school has a Field Day, share your design with the planning committee. They may want to use the course you designed!

GLOSSARY

cross products: the result of multiplying the numerator of each fraction in an equation by the denominator of the opposite fraction. When the fractions are equivalent, the products are equal.

cylinder(s): a three-dimensional geometric figure with two parallel sides that are equal in size and a curved edge.

dissolves: to join a liquid to become a solution.

double number line: two number lines that show a relationship between two sets of numbers.

equation: a number sentence that shows that two mathematical expressions are equal.

equivalent: mathematical expressions that have the same value.

javelin: a lightweight spear.

meteorologist: a scientist who collects and analyzes data to predict weather.

Northern Hemisphere: the area on the globe above the equator.

order: to put values in order from least to greatest or greatest to least.

parallel: objects, such as lines, that are side by side but never touch.

proportion: an equation that shows two equivalent fractions.

radar: a system that sends out pulses of radio waves to find out where an object is or its direction or speed.

rates: ratios that compare two different units, such as miles per hour.

ratio: a comparison of two numbers using division.

round: to find the nearest whole number or the nearest cent in a decimal number.

satellites: objects that revolve around another object. Satellites orbit Earth, collecting and sending information.

slalom: to move in and out around obstacles, such as poles on a ski slope.

surge: a change in sea level caused by storms.

table: a chart used to show relationships between sets of numbers.

thermoplastics: sticky substances found in nature, such as plant sap, that become plastic when heated and harden when cooled.

unit rate: a rate with a denominator of 1, such as $\frac{10 \text{ feet}}{1 \text{ second}}$.

FURTHER READING

FICTION

Hurricane: A Novel, by Terry Trueman, HarperCollins, 2008

NONFICTION

Get Outside: The Kids Guide to Fun in the Great Outdoors, by Jane Drake and Ann Love, Kids Can Press, 2012

Go Out and Play!: Favorite Outdoor Games from KaBOOM!, by KaBOOM! Staff, Candlewick Press, 2012

ADDITIONAL NOTES

The page references below provide answers to questions asked throughout the book. Questions whose answers will vary are not addressed.

Page 7: $\dfrac{6 \text{ feet}}{\text{second}}$

Page 12: $\dfrac{60 \text{ feet}}{20 \text{ seconds}} = \dfrac{3 \text{ feet}}{\text{second}}$

Page 13: $\dfrac{100 \text{ yards}}{45 \text{ seconds}} = \text{about } \dfrac{2 \text{ yards}}{\text{second}}$

Page 15: $\dfrac{40 \text{ yards}}{20 \text{ seconds}} = \dfrac{2 \text{ yards}}{\text{second}}$

Page 17: $\dfrac{10 \text{ tosses}}{10 \text{ seconds}} = \dfrac{1 \text{ toss}}{\text{second}}$

Page 18: $\dfrac{100 \text{ yards}}{85 \text{ seconds}} = \text{about } \dfrac{1 \text{ yard}}{\text{second}}$

Page 19: $\dfrac{80 \text{ feet}}{75 \text{ seconds}} = \text{about } \dfrac{1 \text{ feet}}{\text{second}}$

Page 20: $\dfrac{2 \text{ inches}}{2.5 \text{ minutes}} = \dfrac{0.8 \text{ inches}}{\text{minute}}$

Page 21: $\dfrac{104 \text{ yards}}{52 \text{ seconds}} = \dfrac{2 \text{ yards}}{\text{second}}$

Page 22: $\dfrac{60 \text{ feet}}{20 \text{ seconds}} = \dfrac{3 \text{ feet}}{\text{second}}$

Page 23: $\dfrac{16 \text{ captures}}{4 \text{ minutes}} = \dfrac{4 \text{ captures}}{\text{minute}}$

Page 24: $\dfrac{9 \text{ yards}}{12 \text{ seconds}} = \dfrac{0.75 \text{ yards}}{\text{second}}$

Page 30: $\dfrac{60 \text{ yards}}{2 \text{ minutes}} = \dfrac{30 \text{ yards}}{\text{minute}}$

Page 31: $\dfrac{75 \text{ feet}}{120 \text{ seconds}} = \text{about } \dfrac{0.6 \text{ feet}}{\text{second}}$

Page 33: $\dfrac{9 \text{ items}}{9 \text{ seconds}} = \dfrac{1 \text{ item}}{\text{second}}$

Page 35: $\dfrac{40 \text{ yards}}{16 \text{ seconds}} = \dfrac{2.5 \text{ yards}}{\text{second}}$

Page 36: $\dfrac{200 \text{ yards}}{200 \text{ seconds}} = \dfrac{1 \text{ yard}}{\text{second}}$

Page 38: $\dfrac{15 \text{ pounds}}{30 \text{ minutes}} = \dfrac{0.5 \text{ pound}}{\text{minute}}$

Page 39: $\dfrac{80 \text{ yards}}{4 \text{ minutes}} = \dfrac{20 \text{ yards}}{\text{minute}}$

Page 41: $\dfrac{80 \text{ yards}}{160 \text{ seconds}} = \dfrac{0.5 \text{ yards}}{\text{second}}$

Page 44: $\dfrac{15{,}240 \text{ feet}}{3 \text{ hours}} = \dfrac{5{,}080 \text{ feet}}{\text{hour}}$

INDEX

CONTENT CONSULTANT

David T. Hughes

David is an experienced mathematics teacher, writer, presenter, and adviser. He serves as a consultant for the Partnership for Assessment of Readiness for College and Careers. David has also worked as the Senior Program Coordinator for the Charles A. Dana Center at The University of Texas at Austin and was an editor and contributor for the *Mathematics Standards in the Classroom* series.